Delia Consuegra de Sucre

Computer Security, Networks and ICT

Delia Consuegra de Sucre

Computer Security, Networks and ICT

Tips, solutions and news

ScienciaScripts

Imprint
Any brand names and product names mentioned in this book are subject to trademark, brand or patent protection and are trademarks or registered trademarks of their respective holders. The use of brand names, product names, common names, trade names, product descriptions etc. even without a particular marking in this work is in no way to be construed to mean that such names may be regarded as unrestricted in respect of trademark and brand protection legislation and could thus be used by anyone.

Cover image: www.ingimage.com

This book is a translation from the original published under ISBN 978-620-2-15951-7.

Publisher:
Sciencia Scripts
is a trademark of
Dodo Books Indian Ocean Ltd. and OmniScriptum S.R.L publishing group

120 High Road, East Finchley, London, N2 9ED, United Kingdom
Str. Armeneasca 28/1, office 1, Chisinau MD-2012, Republic of Moldova, Europe
Printed at: see last page
ISBN: 978-620-7-01082-0

Table of Contents

DANGER IN SOCIAL NETWORKS AND THE INTERNET IN CHILDREN

The internet has become an indispensable part of our daily lives. Adults, young people and children always have a device at hand. Currently, in Panamanian private schools, children are asked to bring their own device to facilitate the teaching-learning process. ITU and UNESCO studies confirm that more than 50% of the world's population has access to the Internet and 30% of potentially active users are children.

As expressed by Piedrahita (2020), social networks have allowed the immediacy of information and have revolutionized the knowledge society. We ask ourselves: Are our children safe surfing the Internet?

WHO estimates that 200 million children are sexually abused each year. And increasingly, much of this abuse takes place online or is recorded and distributed digitally.

Computer crimes against children are becoming more and more frequent. Cyberbullying, cyberbullying, grooming, sexual exploitation of children through videos, photos, child pornography, publication of private information, sextortion, etc. How can we teach our children to protect themselves on the Internet? Tell your child to show you: What does he/she do, who are his/her friends, and what does he/she use the networks for?

Once they log in, you can teach them how to set up privacy settings and warn them how important this is. It is common for children to put everything on the public wall, because they believe that everyone who connects to the Internet is like them, that they are their friends. Their naivety does not allow them to imagine that there are perverse personalities or that they seek to connect with children and adolescents for other purposes. The advantage of setting privacy is that only his friends will access what he publishes.

It is very important that you point out to your child that serious computer crimes are committed because of information provided by a family member on social networks. Quoting Cortez (2019), through Social Engineering, the person behind the computer interrogates the child or adult without the child realizing that he or she is extracting important information from the home. When children upload a photograph, a video to a social network or a blog, anyone can capture it, save it on their cell phone or computer and upload it to another website or social network; then, it would be impossible to remove that photo that we did not want to publish and it will be circulating everywhere in the world and we lose control over it.

There are many parents who deny their children the use of social networks, forbid them to upload photos to the web and try to explain to them about the dangers of the network, but curiosity is the engine of learning that leads them to explore, especially when they say: "all my friends have it" and I wanted to know what it was like to be on Facebook; and they do it on the sly, although the policies of many social networks do not allow minors to register, children lie and place that they are over 18 years old. Then, as parents, the only thing left for us to do is to teach them, warn them and help them to analyze the information, photos and videos that do not show situations or places that lend themselves to tempt criminals.

We hope that this method is more effective and that they learn to open their eyes in the virtual world, since we cannot stop it, it is here to stay, and that they apply the computer security that each social network has, carefully reading the privacy policies of each application.

According to Unesco (2019), in 2018, the U.S. National Center for Missing and Exploited Children received 18.4 million reports of online child sexual abuse material. Seventeen percent of parents claimed that their children had been victims of cyberbullying. In some countries, that number rises to 37%.

The World Health Organization (WHO) estimates that 200 million children are sexually abused each year. And increasingly, much of this abuse takes place online or is recorded and distributed digitally. In this case, the internet facilitates abuse and exploitation.

As adults we must be aware that a cybercrime is just around the corner, with a little click of the mouse, with online pedophiles, live filming of minors, while abusing them in real time. Usually, the people abusing a minor are not strangers, it is someone they trust, and the child keeps silent. A photograph is the first step, for child abuse, it is only a matter of time.

Cybercriminals use encryption systems to hide their IP addresses, infiltrate chat rooms, gain the trust of our children through anonymity and nicknames. It is the job of adults to find a way to mitigate and prevent the harms and risks children face when they are online.

ATTACKS AND VULNERABILITIES IN BLUETOOTH COMMUNICATIONS

> *All of us who have had a smartphone in hand have at some point in our lives been asked to activate bluetooth to pass information, music, video or document to someone.*

All of us who have had a smartphone in hand, at some point in our lives we have been asked to activate bluetooth to pass information, music, video or document to someone. This has been reduced a bit with the use of email, cloud computing, WhatsApp, Telegram and other applications, but there are still many people who prefer to pass information via bluetooth so that it passes directly and only remains in the 2 devices that are making the connection.

Sony defines Bluetooth as a short-range wireless technology that enables wireless data communication between digital devices, such as a computer or digital camera. This technology works to establish a connection between 2 devices within a range of approximately 10 meters.

The Bluetooth standard is internationally supported and used by thousands of companies worldwide. It can be used inside bags and pockets. But, have you ever wondered, is it safe to use this wireless technology? When we get into our cars, the first thing many people do is turn on Bluetooth, to avoid being with the phone in our hand answering calls we turn it on to listen to music from YouTube or Spotify. But, when you get out of your car, do you deactivate the bluetooth? Or do you usually run errands, work all day and when you head home your cell phone immediately connects to the bluetooth in your car? Currently, there are Smart tv and bluetooth headsets, are you sure (a) that your conversations are not being heard by someone else? According to (Serrano, 2019), the vulnerability of bluetooth wireless communication depends specifically on the bluetooth version in the security of communications between devices, such communication is as strong, as is the weakest link.

Let's talk a bit about these versions to reference (Serrano 2019):

In bluetooth 1.2 version when performing pairing of devices that rely on static unit keys, the attacker can listen to the connections of the original device and impersonate the primary device or anyone connected to it.

In version 2.1 + EDR the key flow is repeated every 23.3 hours there the attacker can decrypt all messages on the connection.

In version 2.1 and 3.0, it allows you to connect to devices that are not compatible, allowing you a faster, but more vulnerable connection.
In versions prior to 4.0 the number of authentication challenge requests is unlimited, so an attacker could collect many responses to obtain password information. Its encryption is considered weak.
Now let's talk about what happens in all versions: if the link keys are not stored properly, an attacker could see them and even modify them, this can lead to a multitude of attacks against the device and anyone connecting to it.
In all versions there is no user authentication, there is only device authentication. The problems that Bluetooth has always had are largely due to the pairing process between devices. Bluetooth can be subject to many attacks, for example:

- **Eavesdropping** (passive eavesdropping of information traffic exchanged between two Bluetooth devices).
- **MAC Spoofing Attack** (the attacker can impersonate legitimate users. This malicious user can start and terminate connections, intercept information and modify it).
- **PIN Cracking Attack** (attacker uses sniffer and E22 brute force algorithm to achieve the matching).
- **Man In The Middle** (the attacker stands in the middle of both legitimate devices and when they believe authentication between them has been successful, they are actually both paired with the attacker).
- **Bluejacking** (a malicious user sends unsolicited messages to a device with bluetooth open, in order to trick the user into replying to the message or saving it to their contacts).
- **Bluesnarfing** (exploiting vulnerabilities in the firmware of older devices, so that an attacker can access data stored on the victim's device such as calendar, calendar).
- **Bluebugging** (the attacker listens to calls, until all the information is extracted from the victim's device).
- **Denial of Service** (an attack characterized by draining the victim's battery due to excessive packet sending).
- **Fuzzing Attack** (sending malformed data to the device's radio interface in order to observe the victim's behavior, slow down its operation, or paralyze its operation).

- **Blueborne** (the attacker can hijack Bluetooth connections, if you have bluetooth enabled devices, simply with the above information, those devices would be potentially vulnerable to attack).

  Have you ever wondered what kind of Bluetooth version your mobile device has?

SOCIAL ENGINEERING AND NETWORK SECURITY

Attacks are increasing daily, cybercriminals' strategy involves a lot of research work, as they first collect as much information as possible from social networks and then register on a platform by creating fake profiles on Facebook, Twitter, LinkedIn and Instagram.

Today, the Trojan Horse scenario can be presented through social networks. Since they have become an essential, fundamental and at the same time responsible part for people, in a space where they make visible all the information about their tastes, needs and personal life problems. And there the attacker takes advantage to persuade and reach them using misleading advertising, that users can not resist and fall into the trap as then, in the city of Troy.

It often involves deceiving victims to gain their trust and get them to break normal security procedures. These procedures open the doors to attackers of their own free will.

Social engineering attacks have been increasing day by day, the strategy used by cybercriminals involves a lot of research work, which leads to be increasingly efficient and with better results, the efficiency of this modality is applied by various means, the attackers first collect the possible information by extracting it from social networks, then the attackers are registered on platform creating fake profiles on Facebook, Twitter and LinkedIn and Instagram.

The other thing they do, is that they consolidate a plan of attack to convey reliability, collect particular information, understand their behavior. For example: topics of interest, friends, likes and dislikes and gain their trust.

The attacker makes his first approach having already defined the tactic of deception he is going to use. When the victim considers him to be a friend, the attacker becomes close and always tries to get even more information out of him by means of lies. Once they are friends, the cybercriminal usually asks for more personal data such as e-mail, address, telephone number.

The identity could be supplanted in a fast and efficient way, a striking link would be sent through email so that you can open it and run a Trojan virus that infects the computer and gives access to all bank accounts of the victim, after getting what he wanted the attacker deletes all traces, leaves profiles and does not speak to the victim again.

According to Romero Rubio, D. A. (2019). Social engineering can be defined as the practice of obtaining confidential information. In most cases information of great value through the manipulation of people's minds, where the attackers by means of deception try to obtain sensitive information or privileges in some system. In short, the aim is to deceive and confuse the user of the computer system so that they end up doing something they do not really want to do, such as running software, providing their passwords or accessing certain services.

There are different types of social engineering attacks. They act on two levels, the physical (descriptive) and the psychosocial (with the method of deception).

This type of attack is very simple, but at the same time quite effective as it can get information in a very short time, compared to other sophisticated hacking techniques. Social engineering can be presented interacting with machines, software and human based.

Perhaps many are wondering how can we eliminate social engineering? I can only say that it is not possible, what we can do is to mitigate the threats, we will always be exposed to this attack technique and the best way to avoid it is not to be fooled, since, at all stages of our lives, we will meet people of all kinds where some wanted to help us get ahead, others want to take advantage of our humility to take advantage of any situation.

I want to leave a very representative phrase and perhaps many of you heard it from information specialists which is "our mind is the weakest link of our being and at some point in our lives, we were or will be puppets".

Social engineering attack techniques are very varied and there are different modalities, acting on two levels, physical and psychosocial. The physical describes the resources and means by which the attack is carried out and the psychosocial is the method by which the victim is deceived.

Plazas García, E. R. (2018). He states that it has been possible to establish that 97% of computer attacks are not derived from failures or vulnerabilities in information systems, but are caused with the use of social engineering techniques with which it is possible to obtain different access credentials to violate computer security and confidential information of people.

It is important to point out that the human mind, as well as being the greatest tomb of secrets, can also be the largest open window of sensitive, important and relevant information for a company or for your life itself, thus providing everything that leads to achieve the dark objectives of an attacker and that is why we must be careful when interacting with strangers and providing relevant information to others.

LET'S TALK ABOUT HACKERS

According to the Real Academia Española de la Lengua, hacker is a "Person expert in the handling of computers, who deals with the security of systems and develops improvement techniques".

The various classifications of hackers are conflated with cybercriminals and used to denigrate them, thus creating in a person without much knowledge of the subject, the misconception that hackers are engaged in crime.

For years, we have been led to believe that a hacker is a hacker, in short a criminal.
When we see news like "graphic designer robs a bank", it does not produce the same impact as if we read "famous hacker robs a bank".
To a neophyte viewer hacker and criminal could be the same thing, but the truth is that there is no point of comparison between the two.
Hackers began testing on available sites that were precisely military, official, mostly for the CIA, Pentagon and NASA.
The computer terms that should be used to refer to them are hackers (the good guys) and crackers (the bad guys).
Over the years hackers were classified according to their main skill and recognized as web, database, voice over IP, server, application, ATM and cellular hackers.
There are purists who are hackers for academic purposes, they test controlled environments, they never do it without prior permissions, they create protocols, tools for network testing, they report bugs, they never cause damage in the development of their activities.
The various classifications of hackers are conflated with cybercriminals and used to denigrate them, thus creating in a person without much knowledge of the subject, the misconception that hackers are engaged in crime.
It is important to make clear that a hacker is an expert in the subject in which he works, it is not possible to be a computer network hacker if you are not first an expert in networks. Hackers have different characteristics, they are judicious, dedicated, curious, have a strong passion for discovering, knowing, creating and sharing knowledge, they are upright, their responsibility is related to their actions and adherence to the rules, which means respect for the property of others, in short, they do not intend to cause harm or prejudice as a result of their actions, they are people who work hard to acquire the ability of lateral thinking, they are constantly updated and know in depth everything related to programming and complex systems, is a born researcher who is inclined to

know everything related to encrypted data chains and the possibilities of accessing any type of secure information.

The Samurai code reflects the desirable characteristics of a hacker, one of the most accurate texts globally and we summarize it in the seven basic principles namely: righteousness, justice, courage, benevolence, courtesy, truthfulness, honor and the duty of loyalty, when the person sees this gives to understand that he knows, understands and accepts this code.

We have in the air an image of those hackers who see themselves as information robbers, sober figures who are above the law and below human composure using their superior knowledge of the digital world to exploit and terrorize ordinary internet users.

We can say that there are different types of hackers, the black hat hackers are the bad guys, they break the security of a computer, create viruses, violate the security of computers, crash servers, enter restricted areas infecting networks and taking them over, we can also call them crackers or criminal hackers.

The white hat ones who are the good guys, the ethical ones, are the ones who penetrate the security of systems to find vulnerabilities, focus on securing and protecting technological systems and define themselves as shields that protect a site or other medium, who claim that they are the only ones who should be called Hackers.

Those who play the good guys and bad guys, do not hack for personal gain, nor have malicious intent are the gray hat hacker.

Those who are mobile savvy are the phreaker, the newbie are the newbies who stumble upon web pages, read and run programs.

Those who boast knowledge and skills that they do not possess, nor have any intention of learning, as they download books and videos only for the purpose of storing them we call them lickers.

There are many reasons to hack, a great purpose is that as long as crackers keep appearing, computer security will grow and they will look for different means to protect information.

We want to make it clear that hacker is not the same as hacker, since the latter is a person who illegally accesses other people's computer systems to appropriate them or obtain secret information, while the former is an expert who contributes to security.

What kind of hacker do you consider yourself, would you use Samurai code? I hope I have changed that ambiguous conception you had about hackers and have contributed something to Computer Security.

LOCATION-BASED SYSTEMS IN SMARTPHONES

Have you ever used a real-time locating system (RTLS)?

Most people who acquire a smartphone have used it. We generally use it when we get disoriented, we are in a large shopping mall, in a hospital, in a city we do not know and we have no choice but to resort to this great tool that appeared in smartphones in 1998, so that an ordinary user could use it.

How did Google come to take it over? In 2003 the Rasmussen brothers together with the Australians Noel Gordon and Stephen Ma, created a company related to mapping and in 2004 it was taken over by Google to create a free software based on the Google Maps browser.

And have you seen the blue dot in the app? By pressing on that dot we can see nearby places, know where a person is currently, share our location, save the place where we parked (parking), calibrate the compass of the device or report a problem.

These location systems are used for mass surveillance, for example, the US NSA intelligence and the British GCHQ massively intercept Google Maps queries made from smartphones, anyone using Google Maps on their smartphone is helping to develop GCHQ's mass surveillance systems.

Another example is the U.S. Global Positioning System (GPS), the Russian Global Navigation Satellite System (GLONASS), the worldwide strategic program called Global Navigation Satellite System (GNSS).

There are other hybrid web applications that combine Google Maps data with other sources such as: waze, panoramio, tagzania, wikiloc, wikimapia that are geolocation mashups.

We have always said that we should not forget that technology is not only a means but also a tool to help us solve our problems, but the essence of our need with these systems is to know the location of a person with greater or lesser accuracy and if possible in real time.

The detail is that as an organization we want to easily find a person within our company or simply want to find the position of a fixed asset, for this we use tag devices that have the ability to transmit their location to a mobile device, this tag can be carried on a keychain, in a wallet because it is extremely small, it has a location sensor to determine the physical position of a device within a global reference.

The tag can also be used as a bracelet, necklace or watch to locate a person, fixed asset or pet, as they are lightweight and measure only a few centimeters.
Several companies use tracking systems for productivity purposes, because they reduce travel time, help optimize routes and encourage efficient driving. It is also used by freight forwarding companies and for carrier safety, as these systems immediately detect if something happens to personnel.
According to (García, 2022) this type of localization is intended to be used in the healthcare sector to find all types of machinery that may be urgently needed to perform some activity, such as a mechanical respirator that a patient needs in a certain room in a hospital.
This publication also refers to the location of health personnel and patients, although it emphasizes that this proposal should be carefully analyzed as it would be a partial intrusion into people's privacy.
Google Maps updated in 2020 the covid-19 layer that shows us the number of covid-19 positive patients within 7 days on the map through a label and tells us the location of vaccination centers.
We want to emphasize that this technology is closely linked to wireless networks (Wi-Fi), access points, the Internet of Things (IoT), emerging technologies (5G), GPS, IP location identification techniques, Artificial Intelligence (AI) as geolocation uses data obtained from a computer or mobile device to identify your actual physical location.
These systems provide an information technology solution that determines the location of an object in a physical (geospatial) or virtual (Internet) environment.
It is now possible with the use of these tools to improve and control Internet commerce using geolocation information.
The projected growth in the market for location-based systems during the forecast period [2022-2031] is attributed to its use in various applications such as healthcare, aviation, travel, and hospitality.
It is important to note that these technologies that transform the way we experience the world have brought enormous benefits, but they also lend themselves to criminal activities and this can only be controlled with the implementation of an efficient IT security plan.

TECHNOLOGICAL CHALLENGES "UNIVERSITY OF PANAMA IN TIMES OF PANDEMIC"

The University of Panama (UP) currently has an enrollment of 93,628 students, 311 careers, of which 171 are undergraduate, 140 graduate, 19 faculties, 4385 professors for the first semester 2022 and 277,791 graduates from 1935 to 2020.

Looking back, today we can confirm that the University of Panama, came out ahead in pandemic in the face of all its challenges, since every challenge is an opportunity, virtual education and technology marked a new era for the first house of higher education.

Classes at UP were taught in virtual mode, Casa Méndez Pereira and its regional centers survived this challenge, Dr. Eduardo Flores, rector, approved agreement by extended meeting No. 3 20 of March 11, 2020 of the Academic Council (seven platforms), the options of virtual platforms in the Directorate of Information Technology and Communication (DITIC): Virtual Moodle, Office 365.No. 3 20 of March 11, 2020 of the Academic Council (seven platforms), the options of virtual platforms in the Directorate of Information Technology and Communication (DITIC): Virtual Moodle, Office 365; with the Directorate of Educational Technology (TE): Edmodo, Schoology, Google Scholar, Moodle; with the office of Virtual Environments (OEVA): Virtual Campus -educational.

For more than 10 years, virtual methods have been used for teaching, and the Master's Degree in Virtual Learning Environments (EVA) offered by the Virtual Campus is a clear example.

The UP continued to teach virtual classes in most of the Regional University Centers and on the Campus, the C.R.U. Los Santos was the pioneer in returning to the face-to-face modality, after covid-19, teachers use the platforms as support for their face-to-face classes, since virtuality is here to stay.

A little before the pandemic, the UP offered several technological services for our students, administrative and teaching staff, but these services took great prominence with the arrival of covid-19, for example: "Institutional e-mail, Virtual Secretariat".

The online registration, born in 2013, through the virtual Secretariat of the UP, is the new window from which you can perform administrative procedures telematically as if you were on campus, this service allows students to access all information regarding their student life, procedures such as: change of location, claims of grades, arrears, consultation of receipts, peace and save, credits, English test certification, the student can customize your profile with your photo, follow up and obtain documents.

Since 2021, the UP has had the option of a digital checkbook for all personnel. We would like to highlight that in Pandemic, the IT Department and its regional centers worked through Teleworking and used Virtual Private Networks [VPN] to safeguard the security of the information.

The University of Panama has a Virtual Library, which has databases such as e-book (with more than 150 publishers), Ebsco Host, Dynamed, Proquest. It also has the University of Panama Library System (SIBIUP) and the online catalog, which provides personalized attention to students and teachers.

The institutional e-mail has multiple benefits for our 3 departments, with 1 TB of capacity to store and share data, it offers each user a free license to use it on personal computers.

Service to teachers platform implemented since 2014, all teachers must capture grades via web at the end of the semester, grade claims, certification and various requests made by students.

The evaluation of teaching performance is nowadays done through a system called SISDEP, where all teachers insert evidence of their work during the academic year.

The admission process was carried out virtually, as well as the registration of research, evaluation of performance, thesis, monographs and final graduation papers, and the reception of the data bank for new professors.

The social service, approved by the General University Council on March 2, 2010, is the set of temporary activities that undergraduate and graduate students perform, periodically, within their area of professional training, for the benefit of the communities that require it, giving priority to the most needy classes.

UP's student insurance that protects our students in the academic period is done online, all students must register to be protected with a policy that guarantees the student's safety while attending classes.

The UP has made great strides, through its Upvirtual (Moodle) platform, teachers can offer their face-to-face classes together with the platform that supports these classes.

During the covid-19 pandemic crisis, UP continued to offer virtual classes in most of the Regional University Centers and on the Campus, the C.R.U. Los Santos was the pioneer in returning to the face-to-face modality.

As of this second semester 2022, we all return to the face-to-face mode, and we are left with the great satisfaction that we have overcome a challenge together with technology.

CYBERSECURITY IN PANAMA

Cybersecurity emerges as a mechanism to control cyberrisk.

And we can define it as the set of techniques, procedures and protocols aimed at the protection of information related to users of cybertechnologies. Arroyo et al., (2020).

This protection demands the custody not only of the information itself, but also of all the elements necessary for its proper management. In other words, cybersecurity aims to protect any type of asset or resource of value to a person, company or organization.

Cybersecurity must combine elements of security, privacy and usability in a balanced way.

It is not the same to save information on the hard drive of our home computer, than to store our confidential information in the cloud of your email, in the same way that we connect to the wifi network of any restaurant.

The goal of an attacker is to explore the weaknesses associated with any device within reach (computer, phone, tablet) in order to take advantage of a breach of any of the three security-related objectives: confidentiality, integrity and availability (CID).

In recent years, there has been a lot of talk about cybersecurity in Panama, but How did Cybersecurity come about?

According to the company (TiGO) cybersecurity in Panama requires greater disclosure, promotion and analysis.

The National Council for Government Innovation, approved by resolution No. 21; of March 12, 2013 the national strategy for cybersecurity and critical infrastructure protection, which has pillars such as protecting privacy, preventing crimes in cyberspace, strengthening critical infrastructure, promoting a culture in security, the adoption of standards, etc.

On March 29, 2021, the Personal Data Protection Law came into force in the Republic of Panama by means of Law 81 of March 26, 2019. This Law establishes the principles, rights, obligations and procedures that regulate the protection of personal data in our country for natural and legal persons.

ANTAI is the competent authority to determine whether a piece of information lacks legal basis and is inaccurate.

A study on cyber risk management and information security trends in Latin America and the Caribbean 2019, by Deloitte, shows that 4 out of 10 organizations suffered a cybersecurity incident in the last 24 months.

For Alvarado, C. (2018). "As far as Panama is concerned, the spokesperson for Frontera Security warned that most companies do not have adequate personnel and technology to protect their information in the different states where it is processed and used". According to the specialist, "In Panama we are at a very basic level of maturity in cybersecurity issues".

According to the Public Prosecutor's Office, from 2016 to 2021 there was a 421% increase in cybercrime cases in Panama, which increased by 20% from 2019, without a pandemic, to 2020 with a pandemic.

In 2021, 794 complaints were filed, 68% of which were frauds.

Law 14 of May 18, 2007 of the Criminal Code of the Republic of Panama, in its Title VIII, regulates crimes against computer security "Legal Security of Electronic Media".

Panama was the second Latin American country, after the Dominican Republic, to ratify the Budapest Convention, since Law 79 of October 22, 2013 approved the Convention on Cybercrime, published in Official Gazette 27403-A of October 25, 2013.

Some organizations have been created to provide support, in 2011 CSIRT, an agency of the National Authority for Government Innovation (AIG). CSIRT-Panama is responsible for preventing and identifying attacks and security incidents to the country's critical infrastructure computer systems. In such a way that users are alerted in time.

The IDB (Inter-American Development Bank), in 2021, published a report on cybersecurity 2020 entitled "Risks, Progress and the Way Forward in Latin America and the Caribbean", where it states that Panama, Brazil, Uruguay, Colombia and other countries have implemented governmental measures against cybersecurity threats in the continent, such as developing and implementing national and legal strategies to face cyber threats and discussing strategies on cybersecurity in personal data.

Threats can be caused by an attack or cyber-attack, by some kind of physical incident (fire, flood, etc.) or by a lack of care or negligence in following security recommendations (using a personal flash drive in a work computer). On the other hand, threats can originate from within an organization or from outside.

Accenture's (2019) report states that, over the next five years, private sector companies risk losing around $5.2 trillion due to cyberattacks, which is almost the size of the economies of France, Italy and Spain combined.

EDGE COMPUTING

It is a technology that will define and revolutionize the way humans and devices connect to the Internet.

This technology will make the cloud and the Internet of Things [IoT] better than they are today.

It is a type of computing, which occurs at or near the physical location of the users, at or near the data source, allowing users to have fast and reliable services.

Before understanding Edge Computing we must understand what is cloud computing, known as cloud computing, is the technology capable of storing and processing all our files and data on the network, without the need to do it on our devices. Example: every time you upload a document, photo, video to platforms such as instagram, facebook, dropbox, one drive, google drive, icloud.

We use cloud computing on a daily basis, perhaps without even realizing it, because we use e-mails, access our bank accounts, use social networks and every time we do this, we are making use of cloud computing.

To access the cloud and edge computing all devices must have a fixed or wireless internet connection, that internet provider is responsible for getting your data from your device to a destination server using an IP address or a web address, to identify the site to which the information should be sent.

When you connect to Gmail through one device it asks the Google server to show you your inbox, as the data is in the cloud, it will show you the same thing on all your devices, all this requires a series of protocols, every time you connect, your data makes a journey through the network.

The internet of things [IoT] is the system made up of thousands and thousands of devices, machines and objects interconnected to the Internet, there are multiple objects that connect to the internet of things, including: Alexa, Siri, Cortana, Google Now, Google home, Tesla cars, speakers, smart plugs, thermostats. This information is stored and processed in large data centers, this technology can become very expensive and consumes a lot of energy.

The possibilities that can be gained by bringing the cloud closer to where the data is generated are incalculable.

Edge Computing is about bringing the processing power as close as possible to where the data is being generated, in other words, it is bringing the cloud closer to the user, to the very edge of the network, bringing the ability to process and store data closer to the user.

Processing happens much closer, speed is faster, latency is reduced and possibilities are multiplied.

There is already talk of new generation networks (5G and fiber optics) they offer very high latency reductions, which is the time in which the information takes to go to the server and 4G networks offer an approximate latency of 50 milliseconds, with 5G and fiber that figure can go down to 1 millisecond.

Edge computing creates a mesh network of micro data centers that literally brings the cloud closer to the user, significantly reducing latency.

Edge computing provides more security, privacy and increases the quality and reliability of data processing, characteristics that are enhanced when communicating with flexible networks, highly adaptable to the needs of each moment and in which artificial intelligence is already present.

How does edge computing benefit users and businesses on a day-to-day basis?

Edge computing is related to machine learning, as they offer automatic learning models, which work by training artificial intelligence [AI] with thousands of thousands of images, the AI ends up learning which are the characteristics of the elements that do not present defects and, if they fail in a specific one, it determines that it has not passed quality control.

Edge computing is connected to the car of the future, which includes cameras and sensors that capture information about the environment in real time and can be connected to the traffic network of a smart city.

Using the power of the cloud, Edge Computing connects to video games where every time a button is pressed, the information from that press travels to the server, is processed and returned.

"Remember: before upgrading your operating system, check the memory, hard disk, graphics card and processor of your PC to avoid inconveniences, expenses and technical problems."

In companies, 5G surveillance drones, which allow real-time monitoring of the progress of infrastructures, e.g. roads or communication routes, without the need to send a technician in person. We are ready to go to the edge of the network, as Edge Computing is just around the corner.

MY PC IS ASKING FOR WINDOWS 11 UPGRADE'

For users of the Windows family, it is very common lately for computers within their updates to request an "upgrade to Windows 11".

Most of the users click on upgrade "without thinking about it", since they consider that it is the best for our devices, without knowing whether or not their equipment has the minimum specifications or hardware requirements for the installation of this new operating system.

When Microsoft announced the arrival of Windows 11 it was very clear and specific, warning that the requirements of the operating system would be exclusive.

First of all, as users, we must check if our equipment is suitable for updating, downloading and running the operating system.

In Microsoft's web page we can find the characteristics, specifications and necessary requirements for its installation, which requires a minimum memory of 4GB, a processor of 1 GHz or faster with two (2) or more cores (this is a determining factor for the execution of Windows 11).

The hard drive must have a minimum capacity of 64GB and the graphics card must support DirectX 12 or later with the WDDM 2.0 driver (graphics display driver). DirectX 12 is a set of Windows components that allows the main "software" and games to work directly with the audio and video "hardware". In games it is used to enhance the overall multimedia experience.

It is important that the TPM (system that allows our computer to store keys to encrypt communications, hard disk or provide the security of our equipment) has a version 2.0.

The screen must be in high definition (720p) greater than 9" diagonally, 8 bits per color channel, because if it is less than 9" the Windows interface may not be visible.

If the computer has Windows 10 it will ask for the update to Windows 11, if not you will find it available in Windows> update> settings> security.

Secure boot can be enabled with UEFI.

Windows 11, requires Internet connectivity and a Microsoft account to complete the device configuration on first use.

Users think that the best thing to do is to update the equipment, but they do not make sure beforehand whether or not the equipment has the minimum requirements, because, just as users install an application without reading it out of ignorance, they do not imagine that this will make their equipment run slower, that they may get blue screens or begin to face certain difficulties as soon as you agree to update the operating system.

All operating systems enter a phase of testing by users or consumers and this is the moment when certain deficiencies come out that go beyond typical errors. We can observe that the graphical environment of an operating system is always more attractive in the eyes of users, but in this case Windows tries to copy that of Apple or cell phones. Windows has a very clean and attractive presentation, it keeps many programs and applications from the past that clash with the new face of Windows.

Windows 11 has a very limited and modern taskbar, as it includes almost all the basic applications for working on the PC.

The Windows 11 start menu is also very limited, they have removed elements from Windows 10 that we all already knew and have not replaced them with other options.

It has unnecessary programs that nobody uses, Windows 10 came with many games that nobody uses at work and professional level, but Windows 11 has come with a number of unnecessary applications for many users, which take up space and can impair in some way the operation of the system.

All operating systems in their initial phase have compatibility, printer and network driver problems.

There are times when users make changes in the "hardware" and we must know if our equipment complies with the features to make updates in the "software", "not everything new is great and perfect".

There are many users who wish to continue with outdated applications and systems, either due to lack of knowledge, lack of economic resources, attachment to their old equipment and are reluctant to upgrade, but before installing any application we must make a correct evaluation of our "hardware", applications and operating systems.

By this we do not mean that Windows 11 is deficient or bad, it is simply demanding in terms of requirements, but they are working on solutions and updates to improve.

Remember: before upgrading your operating system, check the memory, hard disk, graphics card and processor of your PC to avoid inconveniences, expenses and technical problems.

COMPUTER SECURITY TIPS

Computer security attempts to protect the storage, processing, and transmission of digital information. No matter how much effort you have put into building a digital barrier around your computer, you may still wake up one morning to find that it, or a copy of it, has been lost, stolen, or damaged by any series of unfortunate accidents or malicious acts.

We must know that there are very powerful machines, but also very vulnerable. Therefore, I share with you several tips for the computer security of users.

Always keep your operating system updated, operating systems undergo various changes and offer good tools, such as Windows Update, that allow your computer to be updated automatically, the update allows vulnerabilities caused by viruses to be corrected and prevents malicious software from spreading.

> ***"We must uninstall all applications that we do not use and avoid installing pirated software on our computers, because this ends up being a source of vulnerabilities [...]"***

Let's use an antivirus and "Anti-Malware" applications, for the security of our computer equipment it is essential to have an antivirus, in the market there is a range that you can use to protect your computer, only that there are some heavier than others and we must read carefully what are the minimum specifications that requires that antivirus that we want to install for its proper functioning.

It is very important that we use programs to locate "malware", such as "malware bytes", which allows us to eliminate, search for "software" and malicious applications.

Some people use one password for many years for all applications and this represents a risk, because once they discover one, they discover them all, it is very common to arrive at a public office and you can see the little papers stuck on the monitors or desks with the passwords written down to enter the systems, this happens even in financial institutions and it is a great risk for fraud and scams, since the user is leaving everything on his desk.

When you are in public places, click on the forget password option, since most of the intrusions are produced by placing a password easy to guess, for example, the users place the date of birth and the names of their children, because it is an important data and they are not going to forget it easily. In this case we can use "keepass", which is a password manager that allows to protect different passwords securely and supports different operating systems (it is multiplatform).

Activate the "firewall" of your operating system, since all operating systems have a "firewall" that allows the user to select the traffic that enters your computer, preventing certain types of attacks on the network, it is recommended that it is used and activated in a configuration as closed as possible to avoid unwanted access to your computer.

Use software to prevent "ramsonware" (data hijacking), a type of malicious program that restricts access to certain parts or files of the infected operating system, is one of the most pressing threats today, hijacking confidential files and taking control until the victim pays to restore the system to working order.

We must use secure technologies and browsing "software" that allow privacy, for example, in Google Chrome there is the incognito mode, which opens a window independent of the normal Chrome windows. Firefox, allows the use of private browsing mode and that a third party can not exploit. Similarly, we must configure the deletion of data from browsing sessions.

Use backups, this is your backup in case you lose the information that is hosted on your device, operating systems have an automatic "backup" and there are plenty of free programs such as EaseUS Todo Backup Free, Comfortable Backup, IDrive Cloud Backup, Google Drive Backup, Cobian Backup.

Use a VPN (Virtual Private Network) software, which allows us to establish secure and encrypted connections with the companies where we work, in this way all the work we do will be secure, encrypted and will prevent third parties from observing it and stealing information.

It is not recommended to use free VPN, some of them are Hide.me, TunnelBear, Speedify, Opera already has its VPN, Firefox is already starting to use its own, ProtonVPN Free, Windscribe, Hotspot Shield Free VPN.

There are tools to encrypt USB and removable devices, it is important that our removable storage systems, such as hard drives, USB sticks, are encrypted with specific encryption software, so that third parties cannot easily access their content, e.g. Veracrypt, Axcrypt, Bitlocker, Filevault 2, Boxcryptor.

We must uninstall all the applications that we do not use and avoid installing pirated software on our computers, because this ends up being a source of vulnerabilities, since the essential thing is to minimize the probabilities of having future problems.

THE USE OF ICT IN THE INFANTILE AGE

"[...] technology is very good, ICTs came to change the world, the key is to find a point of balance, to avoid the abuse of technological dependence, [...]"

According to psychologist Frederick Skinner, the real issue is not whether machines think, but whether men do.

According to the American Academy of Pediatrics, children as young as six (6) months are already exposed to technology use for at least 30 minutes a day.

Preschoolers are not able to spread a slice of bread with butter, but they are able to watch their favorite videos on YouTube.

With the incorporation of all the technological equipment into 21st century classrooms, there is little question as to whether this is an advance or whether we are stunting childhood with the use of technology.

Every day we see more and more parents offering a mobile device to their children to control them, suppressing children from running, talking, playing, there is no laughter, there is no human warmth, we do not even see an exchange of looks between parents and children.

Our games of yesteryear are lost: can, hide and seek, spinning top, hopscotch, jump rope, jigsaw puzzles, freezing, 1-2-3 bread and cheese, marbles, and soon they will not know what it is to ride a bicycle.

And what happens to those children who cannot yet read and write and are given a technological device?

It has been demonstrated that, when typing, the movements are not the same as holding a pencil in our hands, since it does not allow us to discern between some letters and others.

The scientific method tells us that the habit of writing by hand accelerates the process of learning to read.

An experiment conducted on 14 children aged four (4) and five (5) years tells us that handwriting, making strokes and drawings every day brings great benefits in brain development and activation of the intellect.

Every time we pick up a pencil to go over the letters and words of what we are going to write and hand paint is a treatment for dyslexia.

It is not only saying that children are digital natives and feeling proud of that, the fact is that we are silencing them, throwing them an iPhone, with that iPhone all the problems begin, one of them is believing that, because we were born surrounded by technology, we are competent in its use.

In schools, digital skills must be acquired to enable children to solve various problems with these acquired skills.

Several studies have reported that, although typing on a computer takes less time because it is a faster process, taking notes by hand improves memorization and word recognition for a student.

According to Garay (2005), the knowledge society is characterized by free access to knowledge through ICTs and their reach at various levels of society.

Technological devices are in the classroom and can be key elements for learning, we must be aware that in primary education, these devices diminish student learning, as they are not mature enough to limit distractors and ensure that learning is effective.

When you give a device to a child it is for recreation, because otherwise, without prior adult supervision, everything will become a game.

The key is to find a point of balance, avoid the abuse of technological dependence, avoid problems associated with concentration, self-control and emotion management in our children.

Muhammad Yunus states that: "Technology is important, but the only thing that really matters is what we do with it".

Our children learn by example. It is the parents' responsibility to train that child and teach him/her the proper use of technology, so that he/she recognizes when, how, where and why he/she should use technological devices.

Both in the family and in schools, we must train this child to discover that technology is a valuable and positive didactic resource for his or her education and training.

OPERATING SYSTEM UPDATE

"[...] it is necessary to know that we cannot buy everything that is on the market, [...] unfortunately, this will happen to many users due to lack of knowledge."

Operating Systems

If your computer is about five or six years old, there is a possibility that you may not be able to upgrade to Windows 11. Microsoft's website presents the specifications of the computers that they recommend to be able to upgrade to Windows 11, due to the TPM 2.0 requirement.

What is TPM? It is a small chip located inside the computer, on the motherboard that helps with the security of the computer.

First, Microsoft released the TPM 1.2 for companies, now they are releasing it updated for all users, with the objective that we all have the same level of security and we need to invest in new hardware.

We refer to Windows simply because it is the most widely used operating system worldwide, according to Microsoft the reasons for the strict system requirements are based on performance and to reduce ransomware attacks, ensuring the security of users.

In Windows 11 the TPM is used by BitLocker for data security and Windows Hello for identity protection.

According to Microsoft publications, they have observed a decrease of up to 60% in malware.

Some claim that Windows 11 is faster, while others claim the opposite, in several experiments with high-end and low-end PCs we can see that there are significant performance changes in the "hardware".

Computers have virtualization-based security (VBS) to enhance the security of operating systems, sometimes installed by default.

When VBS is installed it reduces the performance of games by up to 25%. Especially, if it has been installed on Windows 11.

Most people click where it says "upgrade to Windows 10", without knowing that this can slow down the computer, this upgrade with VBS enabled slows down the computer much more than installing Windows 11 from scratch, all tests reveal that the configuration from scratch is optimal.

To investigate if VBS is enabled, we must perform the following steps: Settings, Update and Security, Windows Security, Device Security, Kernel Isolation and disable "Memory Integrity".

By running the PC Health Check tool, we can find out if our computer can run Windows 11.

One of the options to install the new operating system on your computer is to buy a TPM module and insert it in our motherboard, if your computer is prior to 2016 and above 2011, it should have a minimum of a TPM 1.2.

The HWiNFO application allows us to know the model and specifications of the motherboard and thus to know if it has a connector for the TPM module (only applies to desktop PCs).

Most technicians always recommend upgrading Windows, obviously it is the most convenient and on all computers it works correctly, but in Windows 11 we are observing many stability problems after upgrading.

If your computer does not meet the requirements and you think you should not invest in the purchase of a module, stay with Windows 10, as we will have support at least until October 14, 2025, and will give you the option to look for other alternatives or change your computer.

Windows 7 operating system support has been extended until 2020, but some versions have security updates until January 2023.

Support for the Windows 8.1 operating system will end on January 10, 2023.

When computers no longer receive security updates from Microsoft they can become more vulnerable to security risks and viruses.

So, we have two options with Windows: continue using our old computers without security or buy new computers from 2025 onwards, since our suppliers are forcing us to buy new hardware.

But also, it is necessary to know that we cannot buy everything that is on the market, it does not mean that because the equipment is new it meets the specifications required by the new Windows and, unfortunately, this will happen to many users due to lack of knowledge.

A good option is to migrate to free software, systems that are totally free to use, modify and redistribute, software that respects the user's freedom to do what he/she wants with the software.

ALWAYS UNDER SURVEILLANCE, THROUGH OUR CELL PHONE (IA)

They listen to me through Artificial Intelligence (AI).

"Mobile phones listen to us, because we ourselves allow them to, since we do not read the security policies of the applications we download, [...]"

Has it ever happened to you that you are talking about any topic with your friends or family and when you look at your cell phone, magically the topic you were just talking about is there, so you can watch a video or see an advertisement for that product?
We are being watched! You may ask yourself: "Is my cell phone listening to me?
The answer is yes.
The cell phone and all the smart devices you have in your home.
It indicates (Adamssen, 2020) that Artificial Intelligence (AI) is a science with a broad field of study dedicated to the study of the human brain, and allows the development of intelligent programs that act according to sequential algorithms of steps used in computers for the resolution of specific problems and that allow performing activities that are generally performed by the human brain. Particular applications of AI include professional systems, speech recognition and artificial perspective.
Cell phones listen to us, because we ourselves allow them to do so, since we do not read the security policies of the applications we download, every time we install an application we are granting permission to our microphone. When installing an application we must know if the permission it asks for is necessary for the function it will execute in our cell phone.
There are applications that do not need access to the microphone, to the camera, to our contacts and much less to our image gallery, our mobile devices are private, but it is you as a user who accepts and allows more than four things to be done on your device.
This information from our devices has a commercial purpose, it is collected for targeted advertising.
Currently, there are thousands of people in the world talking to personal assistants such as Apple's Siri, which is a voice-integrated personal assistant found on the ipad, ipod touch, Apple Watch, AirPods, HomePod and Mac, it is as if you were talking to a friend

in real time and it helps you do various tasks on your computer, sends messages, makes reservations, etc.

We have Cortana from Windows, Samsung's Bixby, Sara from Post, Amazon's Alexa, solutions based on artificial intelligence supported by technologies such as biometrics that streamline processes and allow us to meet the needs of users.

There are also Chatbots, an assistant that works through an online chat, designed to hold a conversation with preconceived answers and handle pre-structured messages in text mode.

Our phones listen to us because we have installed artificial intelligence software such as personal assistants.

Google explained the operation of its "Ok, Google" assistant, which processes ambient audio while in standby mode to detect if it wants to be activated. If it does not hear the phrase "Ok, Google", those audios are erased.

The same thing happens with Apple, as it listens to Siri logs to check later if the assistant has responded appropriately. To deactivate this consent you must go to privacy in settings, and deactivate the option "Improve Siri and Dictation".

Artificial intelligence continues to develop continuously and is currently applied in different fields, and it also belongs to our daily lives, and most of its applications are aimed at improving and facilitating our lives.

But how can we prevent them from listening to us, by disabling all mobile applications that have access to our microphone, sometimes we install applications and we do not read the security policies and within these policies is the access to our microphone.

Lionel Brossi et al. (2019) states that currently voice virtual assistants are programs supported by artificial intelligence, they possess the ability to recognize language with enormous accuracy and to answer these voice commands, it is a sequence of questions and grounded work with accessible information sources, users have the ability to interact with different platforms by voice.

All programs and applications have IT security policies, which consist of a series of rules and guidelines that guarantee the confidentiality, integrity and availability of information and minimize the risks that affect it.

PORTS, COLORS AND TRANSFER ***RATES***

USB is one of the most widespread and widely used technologies since its emergence in 1996. Its function was to provide the PC with a high-speed external bus that offered the ideal characteristics, defines cables, connectors and communication protocols used in this port or interface. Also known as pendrive. This port has replaced the PS/2, the VGA, the 3.5 mm jack, and the 3.5 mm jack.

This port is used to communicate peripherals with the computer and to power it, just by making the connection it is automatically activated, this is called plug & play.

All USB ports are backwards compatible, they will always work, even if slowly.

In the case of the motherboard, the 3.1 port is usually teal, but it depends on the manufacturer.

Its development continues in order to adapt to the needs of users and to analyze the changes that the world of technology imposes on it in order to profile itself as a technology of the future.

The following are the different types of USB:

USB 1.0 and USB 1.1 are no longer used; USB 2.0 transmits 60 MB/s with Type A and B connectors; USB 3.0 transmits 600 MB/s with Type C connectors; USB 3.1 transmits up to 10 Gbit/s with Type C connectors; USB 3.2 transmits up to 20 Gbit/s with Type C connectors; USB 4.0 transmits up to 40 Gbit/s with Type C connectors; USB Wireless.

The color of the USB port indicates:

Black and white colors, we identify if the interface is 1.0 or 2.0 we want to clarify that today there are no 1.0 peripherals because its speed would be lower than that of a mouse, keyboard, headphones, speakers.

Dark blue color, indicates that the port is 3.0 and transmits 5 Gbps, 10 times faster than 2.0, it is ideal for external hard drives.

Light blue color indicates that the port is USB 3.1 which is 10 Gbps speeds.

We find charging USBs, which are fast charging ports and cables, can transmit more power than normal through increased amperage, while retaining their voltage.

Red color indicates that it is USB 3.2, speeds of 20 Gbps, they are called USB Sleep & Charge, indicates that the connector does not supply charge by suspending, while our equipment is active, our smartphone is charging.

Orange color indicates that the USB 4.0 very similar to the 3.2, but transmits 40 Gbps, the latest technology standard, uses a type C connector the so-called USB-C, which are faster.

Yellow color are always active, even when the computer is not idle or off. Supplies charge even when the notebook is turned off, these ports are always active and powered.

The universal serial bus has helped to standardize various devices and peripherals, for its operation began with the white color 20 years ago, then came out different colors to differentiate the so-called new high-speed bus or a third generation.

The function of the colors is to help us recognize where we should connect the devices in the most appropriate way possible, you will notice that in some ports the access to the information is faster than in others and this happens due to the type and speed of each port.

Our PCs are equipped with the HDMI (High Definition Multimedia Interface) port, a digital interface for transferring uncompressed high-definition multimedia data (audio and video).

The HDMI interface was standardized in 2002 as version 1.0, in May 2004 (version 1.1) and in August 2005 (version 1.2). It is an advanced version of the abandoned DVI port.

In 2007, DisplayPort was developed as an alternative to HDMI, ports that are mainly focused on allowing the connection between computer and monitor, so it is common to find it in displays, as well as in many computer graphics cards.

This connector assists blind people to connect by touch. It supports DisplayPort Content Protection (DPCP) with 128-bit AES, and supports High-bandwidth Digital Content Protection (HDCP) version 1.1 and higher.

WIFI KEY?

In the last 5 years, Panamanian hotel guests have highlighted the importance of wifi connection in their stays.

Nowadays, we hear children, young people and older adults talking about wifi, they all ask when they arrive at a place, What is the wifi key?

As soon as tourists arrive at their destination, they want to have access to a wifi connection to avoid overcharging on their telephone bills.

In the last 5 years, studies that have been conducted on the satisfaction of customers in hotels in Panama have shown that a Wi-Fi connection is of utmost importance in their stay, especially when they are business travelers.

Most business travelers report that not having an adequate wifi connection is the most frustrating aspect of their business trips.

Currently, commercial premises that provide wifi to visitors must perform a detailed analysis of the quality of their connections, since it is useless to have wifi with an inadequate speed, if we have a number of customers who cannot connect or connect intermittently and experience difficulties in enjoying the service, they will not return.

Wifi is derived from "Wireless Fidelity" (Wireless Fidelity) is a system that establishes the transmission of data packets over computer networks, for which uses radio waves propagated in the air, instead of cables we can also say that it is a set of standards for wireless networks based on IEEE 802.11 specifications, which was created in order to be applied in wireless local networks and is currently also used to access the Internet.

We are communicating wirelessly through a myriad of portable devices such as cell phones, printers and everything from game consoles to digital cameras. More and more devices are communicating without the need for wires, allowing us to surf the Internet from anywhere.

As formats evolve and bandwidth and coverage needs grow, new connection types emerge and transmission speeds increase more and more, and quite rapidly, offering a higher quality of connection to users.

In 2021 the standard was approved by IEEE 802.3cu. offering speeds of 100 Gb/s and 400 Gb/s over single-mode fiber at 100 Gb/s per wavelength. The theory is ready, but now we have to find the technologies that make it possible, this change is due to the move from copper to fiber.

IEEE 802 is a set of standards developed by the Institute of Electrical and Electronics Engineers (IEEE) on computer networks, specifically on Local Area Networks (LAN) and Metropolitan Area Networks (MAN).

Dereck Muller tells us that "we tend to think of the Internet as something invisible that is in a cloud, but it is on the Internet where the invisible becomes the visible, where the intangible becomes concrete."

According to Kaspersky (2021), a company dedicated to computer security, 70% of tablet owners and 53% of smartphone owners use public WiFi hotspots.

Through a public wifi-signal they can be easily intercepted, so many laptop and mobile device users put the security of their personal information, digital identity and money at risk.

The public wifi signal is inherently insecure.

In this case it is suggested to request information about your legitimate wifi access point, such as the name and IP address of the connection.

Other recommendations are to use a virtual private network (VPN) when connecting to a public wifi network. This way you will be effectively employing a "private tunnel" that will encrypt all data passing through the network.

In case you need to access your social networks, shopping sites or online banking from your cell phone, it is best to use your cell phone's network.

Computer networks are connected to form the global Internet and countless routers and switches take data from one network and transmit it to another network via real physical cables, which means that it is a network of interconnected networks and that is why we call it the Internet.

SATELLITE COMMUNICATIONS

Satellite communications have been developing over the years.

The first uses of this technology were in the military for voice communications in the early 1960s. Commercial providers were prohibited from building and launching satellites at will. Commercial satellites provide relevant information in areas such as meteorology, geology, environmental science, forestry, and have helped the betterment of any country.

> [...] the Starlink project, which is being developed at a global level, and now reaches Panama, consists of placing satellites in orbit to bring Internet to the most remote places with a high-speed connection".

Satellite communications allow us to reach difficult places, overcome the presence of natural obstacles, allow mobility and dispersion of users, there are large differences between cost and distance, their use is important in civil defense, allow rapid expansion of coverage of existing networks, are ideal for broadcasting and broadcasting systems, residential multicasting, etc.

In 2009, there were 15,000 satellites in orbit and only 2,000 were operating, the rest were pure rubble.

The well-defined path of satellites is known as an orbit.

There are geosynchronous orbiting satellites (GEO), which rotate around the Earth in Earth orbit 24 hours a day.

Medium Earth Orbit (MEO) satellites operate in the 2 GHz frequency range and above.

Low Earth Orbit (LEO) satellites are divided into Small LEO operating in the 800 MHz (0.8 GHz) band, Large LEO operating in the 2 GHz band or above and Mega LEO which translates into higher data throughput and real-time, low-delay video transmission capability.

The communications subsystem of a satellite is essential for the operation of any satellite, because they use different components including: antennas, receivers, transmitters, which must be very secure and lightweight.

Regarding the number of existing satellites, we can say that the USA has around 1897 satellites in orbit. Russia has 146 operational satellites. China has 316 operational satellites. France has 164 active satellites. India has 124 satellites and Spain has 29 operating satellites.

Satellite projects are carried aboard airplanes.

Latin America has not yet mastered launch technology, which is why launches are made from other countries, aboard rockets leased by SpaceX or Soyus.

Brazil, owns and operates 10 satellites, the first one they sent was SGDC in 2017 NanoSatC-Br2 by Soyus to observe space and the atmosphere.

Mexico currently has four satellite orbits assigned by the International Telecommunications Union. Peru has only put into orbit a third satellite called PerúSat1.

Chile, has 3 satellites, orbith, a wholesale provider of high-speed internet services, announced the launch of satellite broadband for underserved areas of Chile.

Argentina has 2 satellites and they want to launch one in 2023 to help universalize internet in the country.

Paraguay, which has 2 satellites, launched its first satellite GuaraniSat-1, a Paraguayan-Japanese satellite in 2022.

In 2020, Japan's Jaxa also partnered with Guatemala to send the country's first satellite, the Quetzal-1 cubesat.

According to reports from the National Authority for Government Innovation (AIG), the Starlink project, which is being developed globally and is now coming to Panama, consists of placing satellites in orbit to bring Internet to the most remote places with a high-speed connection.

The SpaceX company wants to install about 12,000 satellites in orbit, of which there are currently about 2,400 orbiting at a low altitude so that the connection can arrive more quickly.

There is also Project Kuiper, Amazon's plan to launch 3236 satellites in a constellation that aims to offer low-latency, high-speed Internet around the world.

Once the Kuiper System is operational, it promises to provide the Internet to individual consumers as well as to businesses and government agencies. Amazon Web Services, meanwhile, will be responsible for providing the networks and infrastructure to serve customers.

Both projects are ambitious and want to achieve the same purpose, thereby encompassing total planetary coverage, to bring the Internet to places where it has not yet reached.

RANSOMWARE AND ENCRYPTION TOOLS

What is ransomware? According to IBM, ransomware is a type of malicious "malware", or "software", that locks a victim's data or computing device and threatens to keep it locked, or worse, unless the victim pays a ransom to the attacker.

In 2021, 21% of all cyberattacks were ransomware attacks, at which time they demanded money to unlock data on a computer. In the IBM Security 2022 publication we are told that attacks have increased to double and triple extortion, which adds the threat of denial of service (DDoS) attacks that are increasing every day.

Encrypting ransomware encrypts personal files and folders, the original files are deleted once encrypted, you may only discover the problem when you try to access a file, some types of encryption software display a lock screen.

The question is asked: "should I pay for the ransom? The answer is: "it is not recommended", because most of the time the problem is not solved and cybercriminals will continue to look for ways to breach systems, to collect money and cause more infections.

When do these attacks occur? When we visit insecure and fraudulent websites and download files and programs, these "malware" are attached during the download process.

The infection will not be obvious to the user, as it acts in the background, until the data is locked and the ransom is requested.

Ransomware attacks use various methods to infect computing devices or a network, the most prominent of which include:

- Phishing emails and other social engineering attacks: the user is manipulated into downloading malicious attachments.
- Operating system and software vulnerabilities: can inject malicious code into a device or network.
- Credential theft: they steal credentials from authorized personnel, buy them on the black market or use brute force and then use remote access "software" to gain access to the computer.
- Other malware: they develop malware for other attacks and insert ransomware into devices.
- Drive-by-downloads: use websites to pass ransomware to computers without the users' knowledge.

In 2016, the initiative was born to create a platform to join forces to jointly fight against ransomware attacks, and from there arose the "No More Ransom" project, which provides free tools to decrypt hijacked files, focuses on educating users, and provides us with an easy way to make reports when we are victims of an attack.

To decrypt a ransomware with this platform, all we have to do is download the tool and run it, and decrypt all the files so that we can use them.

On the nomoreransom.org website we can see several ransomware decryption tools such as: Aurora, Aura, Bart, Bitcryptor, Chaos, Cry9, Democry, ElvisPresley, Fury, Globe, gogoogle, Hakbit, Jaff, AES_NI, Alcatraz Locker, Babuk, CrySiS, CryptoMix (Offline), 777 Ransom and others.

Let's apply the following steps for risk mitigation:

We must keep the operating system and applications of personal and corporate devices up to date.

Restrict remote desktop protocol (RDP), we must conduct penetration testing on a regular basis, monitoring data exfiltration provides visibility into what data is at risk of exposure.

Use complex passwords and modify them regularly (uppercase, lowercase, number and characters), manage the use of privileged accounts, this will not allow users to install or run unauthorized "software", each one must have an access permission.

Install applications only from trusted sources, implement measures such as disk encryption, inactivity timeouts, private screens, strong authentication, Bluetooth disabling, and control and encryption of removable devices (e.g. USB devices).

Be wary of accessing public wifi networks, provide your employees with cybersecurity training and education.

Enable local firewalls and disable Windows PowerShell if you do not use it, because some ransomware variants use Powershell to run.

The general recommendation of the No More Ransom partnership led by McAfee, Politie, Europol and Kaspersky is not to pay the ransom. Sending your money to the cybercriminals will contribute to the continuation of the ransomware, and there is no guarantee that you will receive the key after payment.

CISCO NETWORKING AND THE FUTURE OF NETWORKS

According to the International Telecommunication Union (ITU), telecommunication is formally defined as any transmission, emission or reception of signs, signals, images, sounds or information of any kind transmitted by wire, optical, radioelectric or other electromagnetic systems.

Molina Robles, F. (2015) points out that a data transmission network is a structure formed by certain physical (actual devices) and logical (transmission and control programs) means developed to meet the communication needs of a certain geographical area.

It is, therefore, a support that allows the connection of several computers (or any other electronic device), in order to provide them with the possibility of exchanging information. We can say that, the world is rapidly covered by networks that allow interconnection and transmission between digital devices, this is equivalent to a digital transformation, which provides the innovation of the industry.

Today we have sensors everywhere, transmitting and collecting large amounts of data in a second. There are different types of networks characterized by function, purpose, geographical size, number of devices.

Sensors are connected to controllers via a wireless connection, controllers collect data and send it for analysis and storage, can make decisions immediately and act together with devices called actuators, which are the ones that take the electrical input and transform it into the physical action input.

The future of networks revolves around artificial intelligence (AI) and intent-based networks (IBNs), as networks connect billions of sensors and have the ability to make changes to physical environments, without human intervention.

Cisco Networking relies on an intent-based network model to simplify the way you connect and protect your users, devices, applications, and workloads from anywhere.

The rise of networking is driven by the sharp increase in remote work and the adoption of hybrid cloud which demands a SASE (secure access service perimeter) strategy, with traditional networks many adjustments must be made manually to meet business requirements and sometimes this leads to errors and delays and less than optimal network performance.

Internet of Things (IoT) devices, cloud-based services and dynamically responsive remote offices are desired to be deployed, the industry has taken steps to create a systematic approach to link infrastructure management with business intent and this is known as intent-based networking.

These intent-based networks harness the power of artificial intelligence, automation, and machine learning to control the function of a network to achieve a specific purpose or intent, allow the team to specify in plain language what they want the network to do, and the network makes it happen.

The network is able to translate intent into policy and use automation to implement appropriate configurations needed throughout the network.

Intent-based networks have key elements such as:

Assurance: is the end-to-end verification of the behavior of the entire network.

Translation: the ability to apply business intent to the network configuration.

Activation: occurs after the intent has been specified and the policies have been created.

Intent-based networks create an agile, responsive network capable of meeting all business requirements.

Cisco Digital Network Architecture (Cisco DNA) is an example of an intent-based network.

It is an open architecture, is executed by software, reduces risks and costs, and simplifies and accelerates operations.

The future of our networks are intent-based networks as they are intertwined with artificial intelligence and machine learning, integrating IoT devices, cloud-based services and remote offices in a way that is relevant and responsive to businesses.

DIFFERENCES AND MYTHS ABOUT YOUR COMPUTER'S HARD DISK

"There are certain myths regarding hard drives, we want to clarify that these myths depend on the hard drive your equipment has."

The hard disk is a storage device where the operating system normally resides, the information is nested on the surface of metal plates, which are enclosed in a casing, it contains mechanical and electronic parts, its recording system is magnetic and digital, the access to the information is random. Older disks are called HDD (non-volatile data storage device).

Nowadays, we hear many people talking about SSD disks (solid state drives or devices), it would not be correct to call them this way, since physically there is no disk or heads or anything that rotates or moves, these disks are based on the same technology as flash memories, this type of memories incorporates a SATA interface, which makes it compatible with this type of devices, which can be replaced by another connector on the motherboard using the same cables.

There are certain myths regarding hard disks, we want to clarify that these myths depend on the hard disk you have in your computer.

Myth No. 1. Formatting the hard disk makes it go faster.

What makes our disk work faster is the installation from zero of the operating system, in many occasions it is more effective and operative to defragment the hard disk.

Myth No. 2. If you download files and information from the Internet you will reduce the life time of the disk.

The wear and tear of recording information is not significant, because the disk is always in operation.

Myth #3. The disk has damaged sectors due to pin landing.

Typically, the number of bad sectors will increase as the disk is used.

Myth #4. Formatting reduces shelf life.

There is no danger of damage to the disk, because the read-write heads are not in contact with the platter surface.

Myth No. 5. Defragmenting the disk damages the head.

When you defragment a disk it causes a benefit on HDD disks, because the information will be contiguous. On SSDs they are not defragmented, it is not key to performance. In SSD disks, it does not work like that, because they access the information through "software" and not through "hardware", as it happens in HDD, because they do it through a needle.

Myth No. 6. Power outages cause damage to the sectors (This myth is half-baked). Older disks (HDD) do not have the anti-blackout system, but modern disks (SSD) do have this protection.

We found certain differences between SSD and HDD, one of these big differences is in the capacity; the SSD has a capacity between 256 GB to 4TB, while the HDD ranges from 1 to 24TB.

SSDs have lower power consumption than HDDs, while HDDs are more economical.

Fragmentation can occur on HDDs, but SSDs do not have fragmentation.

Because they have moving parts, HDDs are much noisier and cause slight vibrations.

As for the durability of the disks, SSD cells can be rewritten a limited number of times, HDDs have mechanical parts that can be damaged by movement.

Booting into the operating system of an HDD takes 16 seconds, while an SSD takes seven (7) seconds.

The data transfer rate for SSDs is 200 to 550 MB/s, for HDDs it is between 50 to 150 MB/s.

The SSD is not affected by magnetism, while in the HDD magnetism can delete data.

One of the advantages of SSD over HDD in durability is that it has a higher failure rate.

After learning about the myths and the most important features, you ask yourself "which drive should I choose?".

If you want a faster computer, an SSD is the way to go, but if you need more storage and don't have enough money, an HDD is the way to go.

In most cases it is convenient to combine both types of hard disk, an SSD as the primary disk (for the operating system) and an HDD as a secondary disk, when the computers are "desktop" for data.

For a laptop, SSDs are recommended over HDDs for speed, durability, boot speed and data transfer speed.

IT SECURITY IN THE DIGITAL AGE

In recent years, we have faced a digital revolution, we all have a computer and mobile devices in our homes and we are connected to computer networks, many people 24 hours a day.

Users are often not aware of the importance of protecting themselves with secure passwords, since we sometimes hear the typical phrase "I don't need to protect myself, because I don't have anything that could be of interest to anyone", anyone can be the target of a cyber attack.

When we talk about information theft, we are talking about personal data, bank accounts, or they can simply use remote access to your computer to commit a crime.

We should all be a bit more careful with the information we handle over the Internet.

We must be cautious in our digital lives, just as we are in our real lives, even if we think that nothing we have is of interest to cybercriminals.

No one leaves the doors of their home open for evildoers to enter, in the digital life we leave our PCs without a good antivirus, antispyware, firewall, antiadware, antispam.

According to Maíllo Fernández, J. A. (2022), a firewall is software that controls the connections to and from my computer, preventing unauthorized people from entering the system.

The purpose of antispyware is to combat so-called spyware programs, which collect information on our computer and send it to the attacker.

Anti-adware is used to prevent the action of computer advertising programs (Pop-up). It is effective in controlling and eliminating unwanted intruders, many of which are not detected by antivirus or firewalls.

We also encounter anti-spammers that are used to prevent spam.

The software we commonly download on the net comes with malware (malicious code) gifts included.

Never share your password with anyone, sharing your password is offering you the key to the door to your digital privacy.

We see in office computers passwords stuck on keyboards, monitors and desktops, because when they turn on their computers every morning they do not waste time looking for them and it is more comfortable for the user, but we are opening the doors of our digital life to ill-intentioned people, who can send a confidential work report, use email, insert a virus, vent your personal life, photos, videos and everything you have on that computer.

If the lock on the door of our home is damaged, we do not hesitate to go to the hardware store and buy a new one, because we fear that a criminal will access and take everything he finds, but if our computer sends us an update, we do not give it the same importance, we even omit the message, those updates that cause us so much inconvenience, are not a simple whim of the programmers, they are to correct bugs, improve compatibility with equipment and collaborate with the user by improving the functionality of the computer.

Users who want to feel secure should keep their computer up to date, from the operating system, antivirus and all software installed on the computer, as many attacks occur from text files that seem harmless.

We should not work with software versions for which the developer has stopped providing support, because these are not updated and are totally exposed to security flaws, without anyone being responsible for a possible solution.

WHAT IS TECHNOLOGICAL WASTE?

Technological waste, according to Arevalo (2017), is the type of waste with the highest presence on the planet, which entails social and environmental risks.

The consumerism of technological equipment has increased in recent years, since they provide comfort and many benefits to human development.

There are Panamanian households made up of three people and each one has two or three cell phones, a laptop, a smart watch, a tablet, at least one desktop computer, a Smart TV, speakers, headphones and everything covered by the word technological device (TD), which is defined as objects that satisfy needs virtually and physically through technology.

According to the 2017-2018 Panama Emprende Report, in terms of ICT Companies operating in Panama, 98 are telecommunications companies, 57 are software development companies, 49 are IT consulting companies and 4 are application installation and integration companies.

Regarding access to the main consumer technologies (Laptops, Desktop, Mobile Telephony, etc.) Internet World Stats, the International Telecommunication Union (ITU), Internet Live Stats and CIA World FactBook, confirm that there was an increase in the use of consumer technologies between 2017 and 2018.

But I wonder: what do you do with technological waste?

Citing Cajamarca (2022), in 2018, approximately 50 million tons of waste were generated. In 2019, 53.6 million tons were processed worldwide, but only 17.4 % is properly recycled. Technological waste is a global problem, as it deteriorates the quality of life and the health of the individuals that make up the ecosystem. It is expected that by 2050, 120 million tons per year will be produced as a result of technological consumerism.

More than 80% of the world's cities do not have policies of responsibility for the use of electronic devices and equipment, and this waste ends up in landfills, streams, rivers, etc.

According to Cavazos (2020), technological wastes contain toxic wastes that represent a threat to human health when they are dumped in open dumps, because they contain mercury, lead, cadmium, arsenic and these substances react when exposed to water, sun, air, resulting very dangerous to health and the environment.

Mercury damages the brain and nervous system, according to National Geographic Spain (2020), lead accelerates mental deterioration and the circulatory system, cadmium can cause infertility and chromium is related to bone and kidney diseases.

A huge problem that exists is the lack of user awareness. The technological recycling process begins when electrical and electronic equipment is discarded, collected, transported for storage and processing; this process culminates when the raw material is obtained to manufacture new electrical and electronic equipment (EEE) and a new introduction is made in the product's life cycle.

Technological scrap can also be repaired, reused and destroyed.

It is recommended to reuse plastics, metals and electronic materials to produce other technological equipment, and in this way we are helping to meet one of the Sustainable Development Goals (SDGs) formulated by the United Nations.

We need responsible users when disposing of their TDs, as this affects all of us on planet Earth and can even lead to death. Let's stop the mania of throwing garbage on the streets and sidewalks.

ENCRYPTION - PRIVACY AND INFORMATION SECURITY

According to the Internet Society, encryption is the process of scrambling or scrambling data so that only someone with the means to transform it to its original format can read it. In other words, encryption takes readable data and alters it so that it appears random, requires the use of an encryption key, and the party receiving the encrypted data must have the correct encryption key to transform the scrambled data back to readable data.

Many people mistakenly believe that encryption, security and the resulting privacy of our data are not that important because we have nothing to hide.

According to Roa Buendía, J. F. (2013), our information and communications era needs encryption more than ever, because there are more and more storage media (portable memories of all kinds) and, above all, more communication mechanisms. People handle a lot of data, which they should not share, e.g. their bank account with their doctor, or details of an illness with their bank manager. We all have information whose privacy is appropriate to maintain under certain circumstances. Encryption has become so integrated into our lives that we rarely think about its impact.

When you review a report, a padlock is displayed in the search bar, indicating that the site uses HTTPS (Hypertext Transfer Protocol Secure), the main protocol used to send data between a web browser and a website. Https is encrypted to increase the security of data transfers.

We use certain chat programs, such as Signal, Telegram, WhatsApp, iMessage, Threema, Facebook Messenger with end-to-end encryption, that means only the person you chat with can read that message.

We connect to our private hotspots through our cell phones to check our email, the hotspot is encrypted, preventing others from using it.

We pay with our credit card which has (3) encryption points: the card chip, the credit card reader and the transmission of credit card information for purchase authorization.

We order food through web applications, such as Pedidosya, Appetito 24, Glovo, ASAP, Bite, Uber Eats, using our cell phones or a computer, the transaction data used to pay online is protected by encryption.

Encryption is a security measure that helps us feel comfortable using the Internet, for example, browsers and websites use HTTPS to provide private and secure communications. The protocols prevent criminals or anyone else from reading our data while it is in transit.

In online shopping and e-commerce, we rely on companies to protect our financial information.

But how does it really work: there are two main types of encryption: symmetric and asymmetric.

With symmetric encryption, the same key is used to encrypt and decrypt data, regardless of whether it is in transit or at rest. If your key falls into the wrong hands, your confidentiality is at risk. We need to send a confidential message, we need to encrypt it, both you and the person sending the message must know the key.

Asymmetric or public key encryption uses pairs of keys, one public and one private, anyone can encrypt a message by encrypting a public key, but only the holder of the private key can decrypt it. Today, most encryption systems are hybrid systems, which use asymmetric encryption to distribute the secret symmetric keys and then use symmetric encryption for their own data.

In end-to-end encryption only the sender and the recipient can read the message, online messages may pass through multiple servers and networks before reaching the recipient and are handled or stored by one or more service providers or third parties. This end-to-end encryption is applied to the message on the sender's device and decrypted on the recipient's device, no device or system in between will be able to decrypt the message.

It prevents potential eavesdroppers including telecommunications providers, Internet providers and even application providers from gaining access to the encryption keys needed to decrypt messages. Users can feel a sense of security knowing that their emails, messages and data are protected against access by unauthorized third parties.

ETHICS IN ICT

For years there has been a lot of talk about ethics, morals and values, from various perspectives, but the world is moving forward radically and it is now up to us to talk about ethics and deontology in ICT.

According to Silva, Neif (2006), information and communication technologies are a set of technological tools that rely on information technology.

According to Bruto, Bibiana (2003), computer ethics is considered as the discipline that analyzes the ethical problems that are created, transformed or aggravated by people who use information technology advances.

The important thing is to use ethics as an instrument of prevention to participate in decision making on technological issues in a stable manner, considering as a foundation the values that are in correspondence with social development.

The task of ethics is to provide guidelines for action when there are no regulations or when the current regulations are archaic.

It is essential to develop an ethics in the use of information technology that involves IT professionals, but the dilemma is: what happens to professionals who misuse technology; they can cause major problems that socially affect many human beings.

There are behaviors that go against human dignity, it is vital for the future of society to educate from an ethical vision. To educate in ethics applied to informatics means to develop values that allow the person to act in a reasoned and autonomous way, to relate to the environment that surrounds us under the principles that make man's life on earth worthy.

The need arises to face the dilemmas that occur as a result of the inappropriate use of technologies, because there are behaviors that imply a close relationship with ethics and morality.

According to Castro, Fidel (2003), it is not only about computing to communicate, but to know, learn, teach and share, he states that: "access to knowledge and culture does not mean by itself the acquisition of ethical principles; but without knowledge and culture one cannot have access to ethics".

Professional excellence is achieved when information technology becomes an instrument at the service of a more human reality.

The idea is that information technology only makes human sense when it preserves the exquisite respect for each of the rights and freedoms in which human dignity is embodied.

Unesco (2008) recommends that in order to live, learn and work successfully in an increasingly complex, information-rich and knowledge-based society, students and teachers must use digital technology and virtualization effectively.

Among the bad practices in the management of ICTs we can mention:

The fabrication or falsification of data and software, plagiarism, intentional bias, abuse in the dissemination of studies, lack of vulnerability tests and remote access control, paying for the preparation of papers and theses, self-plagiarism, using previously published texts without citation, computer attacks by malicious persons or cybercriminals, lack of computer contingency plans, incorrect or omitted citation, use of obsolete technology, ransomware, spyware and phishing attacks, use of known, fixed or saved passwords by default, lack of procedures and controls, failure to back up information, use of a single authentication control, failure to provide timely support to equipment, use of virtual private networks to provide secure access, lack of data confidentiality, child pornography, telephone and web scams, invasion of advertising in social networks, etc.

We must not use our knowledge to harm society. Deontology is the set of norms and rules that require the correct use of computer systems and devices.

Among the commandments of computer ethics developed by the Computer Ethics Institute of Washington are: thou shalt not use a computer to harm other people, thou shalt not interfere with other people's computer files, thou shalt not use a computer to steal, thou shalt not use a computer to give false testimony, thou shalt not use pirated software.

In our country there is a need for the creation of codes of ethics for the various professions, especially in the area of Information Systems, ICT and Computer Science in general.

BIBLIOGRAPHIC REFERENCES

- Álvarez-García, D., García, T., Cueli, M. & Núñez, J.C. (2019). Parental control of Internet use during adolescence: evolution and gender differences. Iberoamerican Journal of Diagnosis and Evaluation, 51, 19-31. https://doi.org/10.21865/RIDEP51.2.02

- Ángel Cepeda, L. M. (2019). Ciberpadres 2.0. seguridad en la red para la familia: (ed.). Editorial Paulinas. https://elibro.net/es/lc/upanama/titulos/133363

- Arévalo Fonseca, S. J. (2022). Computer crime prevention. San Mateo University Foundation. Retrieved from https://elibro.net/es/ereader/upanama/219190

- Arevalo, J. (2017). Simulation of the Gray Line E-Waste Management Process to Plan Future Scenarios. http://repositorio.unsm.edu.pe/bitstream/handle/11458/2629/SISTEMAS%20 - %20Juan%20Carlos%20Arevalo%20Reyna.pdf?sequence=1&isAllowed=y

- Arroyo Guardeño, D. Gayoso Martínez, V. & Hernández Encinas, L. (2020). Ciberseguridad... Editorial CSIC Consejo Superior de Investigaciones Científicas. https://elibro.net/es/lc/upanama/titulos/172144

- Baca Urbina, G. (2016). Introduction to computer security. Mexico City, Mexico: Grupo Editorial Patria. Retrieved from https://elibro.net/es/ereader/upanama/40458

- Bernardes, F.(2010) Children online: risks, opportunities and parental control. https://campus.usal.es/~comunicacion3punto0/comunicaciones/055.pdf

- Betancourt,D. & Palos,P. (2011) Parental Control and Emotional and Behavioral Problems in Adolescents. National Autonomous University of Mexico.

- Budapest. IPANDETEC.ORG. Retrieved from: https://www.ipandetec.org/wp-content/uploads/2018/08/IPANDETECBudapest-final-DD.pdf [February, 2021].

- Brutto, Bibiana Apolonia (2003). Globalización y el nuevo orden internacional: las sociedades de la información, Revista TEXTOS de la CiberSociedad, 3. Available at http://www.cibersociedad.net

- Caizaluisa M, E. (2018). Development of an application for WhatsApp parental control on Android mobile devices. https://repositorio.uisek.edu.ec/handle/123456789/3028

- Cajamarca, D. (2022). Technological garbage, silent environmental pollutant of the XXI century causes and repercussions. Revista Ciencias Técnicas y Aplicadas. Dom. Cien., ISSN: 2477-8818 Vol. 8, no. 2. Special May, 2022, pp. 228-244. DOI: http://dx.doi.org/10.23857/dc.v8i2.2753
- Carrera, X., Beltrán, P. & Villalta, B. (2020). Technology-assisted parental monitoring of adolescents. Hamutay 7(1), 19-27. http://dx.doi.org/10.21503/hamu.v7i1.1906
- Cavazos, B. (2020). You can make a difference. get informed, decide and act! https://monitoreducativo.com/2020/10/17/basura-electronicaproblema-latente/
- Political Constitution of the Republic of Panama (2016)
- Coronel Rojas, C. I. (2018). Safety in children through parental control tools that allow parents to monitor internet use (Doctoral dissertation).
- Costas Santos, J. (2015). Computer security: (ed.). RA-MA Editorial. https://elibro.net/es/lc/upanama/titulos/62452
- Computer Ethics Institute of Washington (2002). The 10 Commandments of Computer Ethics, https://techlandia.com/descripcion-diez-mandamientosetica-informatica-info_395878/.
- Delgado-Zambrano, O. (2023). Implementation of parental control applications in the use of the internet as technological tools to support academic performance. Revista Cátedra, 6 (1), 57-77.
- Durán Rodríguez, L. (2008). Expanding, configuring and repairing your PC: (ed.). Marcombo. https://elibro.net/es/lc/upanama/titulos/35707
- United Nations Children's Fund (2017). State of the world's children. 2017. Children in a digital world. https://www.unicef.es/publicacion/estado-mundial-de-la-infancia- 2017-children-in-a-digital-world
- United Nations Children's Fund (2021). Protecting children's rights in times of crisis. https://www.unicef.org/media/120406/file/UNICEF%20Annual%20Report%2020 21%20 SP.pdf
- Giant, N. (2016). Cybersecurity for the i-generation: uses and risks of the.

social networks and their applications... Narcea Ediciones. https://elibro.net/es/ereader/upanama/46247?
- Hernández Encinas, L. (2016). Cryptography: (ed.). Editorial CSIC Consejo Superior de Investigaciones Científicas. https://elibro.net/es/lc/upanama/titulos/41843
- Internet Society.(2016) Public policy brief: encryption. Retrieved: https://www.internetsociety.org/es/policybriefs/encryption/
- Panamanian Institute of Law and New Technologies (IPANDETEC) (2018). The need to legislate on cybercrime in Panama. https://www.derechosdigitales.org/12378/la- necesidad-de-legislar-sobrecibercrimen-en-panama/
- Kcam-Cubas, JY. (2018). Parental control: from technicality to virtue. [Trabajo Fin de Grado].
- Institute of Family Sciences.
- Maillo Fernandez, J. A. (2017). Sistemas Seguros De Acceso y Transmisión de Datos. Madrid: RA-MA.
- Martínez Ramos, A. (2013). Assembly and maintenance of equipment: (ed.). McGraw-Hill Spain. https://elibro.net/es/lc/upanama/titulos/50226
- Miller, S. (2004). WiFi Security Defend yourself from the new Hackers. Editorial Mc Graw Hills Telecommunications Series.
- Molina, R. (2005) Local Area Networks. RA-MA S.A. Editorial y Publicaciones.
- Morales Alonso, Y. (2020). Parental control in the regulation of the use of social networks in adolescents: influence of social networks in the relationships between adolescents and these. [Final Degree Thesis]. University of La Laguna.
- Montoya,Y. (2018). Beyond parental control: redefining the digital família. https://www.upf.br/_uploads/Conteudo/senid/2018-artigoscompletos/178910.pdf
- Moyano Quicazaque, A, Barahona Martínez, D, Forero Higuera, J and Campos, M. (2017). Analysis of tools used for parental control in mobile devices with internet access. [Final Degree Project] Fundación Universitaria Panamericana.
- United Nations (2019). E-waste, a golden opportunity for decent work. https://news.un.org/es/story/2019/04/1455621

- NATIONAL GEOGRAPHIC SPAIN (2020). The dangers of electronic waste. García, J. (2020). https://www.nationalgeographic.com.es/mundo-ng/peligrosbasuraelectronica_13239

- Panamanian Observatory of Information and Communication Technologies (2019). ICT indicators study. Panama Digital Hub. https://panamahub.digital/es/proyectos/optic

- United Nations Educational, Scientific and Cultural Organization (2019) Child Online Safety: Minimizing the Risk of Online Violence, Abuse and Exploitation. https://unesdoc.unesco.org/ark:/48223/pf0000374580

- UN. (2019). E-waste, a golden opportunity for decent work. https://news.un.org/es/story/2019/04/1455621

- Plazas García, E. R. (2018). Social Engineering in Colombian Companies. [Trabajo Fin de Grado] Universidad Nacional Abierta y a Distancia UNAD. https://repository.unad.edu.co/bitstream/handle/10596/18704/1094921881.pdf;jsessionid=EAFF1FDABBF433B36C9D9887627E2300.jvm1?sequence=1

- Pastor, Y., Martín, R. & Montes, Y. (2018). Patterns of use, parental control and access to information of adolescents online. Estudios Journal. 25(2), 995- 1012. https://revistas.ucm.es/index.php/ESMP/article/view/64821/4564456551630

- Peñalva, A. & Napal, M. (2019). Internet use habits in children aged 8-12 years: a descriptive study. Hamut'ay, 6(2), 55-68. http://dx.doi.org/10.21503/hamu.v6i2.1775

- Royal Spanish Academy (2014). Diccionario de la lengua española (23.a ed.). https://dle.rae.es/

- Red de Agentes Multiplicadores del Uso Seguro en Internet (RIAMUSI).(2019) Manual de uso de Internet. https://www.senniaf.gob.pa/wp-content/uploads/2019/06/Manual-Panam%C3%A1-Validada.pdf

- Cybersecurity Report 2020 Risks, Progress and the Way Forward in Latin America and the Caribbean. iadb.org . Retrieved from: https://publications.iadb.org/publications

- Accenture S.L. Report (2020) Statement of Non-Financial Information. Retrieved from: https://www.accenture.com/content/dam/accenture/final/acom-migration/pdf/pdf-173/accenture-einf-fy20.pdf
- Rivera, R. & Hammersley, C. (2021). Parental mediation cyberguide Tips for responsible internet use by children and adolescents.
- Roa Buendía, J. F. (2013). Computer security: (ed.). McGraw-Hill Spain. https://elibro.net/es/lc/upanama/titulos/50243
- Rodríguez, I. & Sanz, C. (2021) Parental Control: My School with Sanders. [Final Degree Thesis] Universidad Complutense de Madrid.
- Rodríguez, R. & Cantero, M. (2020). Albert Bandura: Impact on education of the social cognitive theory of learning. Padres Y Maestros / Journal of Parents and Teachers, (384), 72-76. https://doi.org/10.14422/pym.i384.y2020.011
- Romero , R (2019). The art of social engineering. Universidad Piloto de Colombia. http://repository.unipiloto.edu.co/handle/20.500.12277/6354
- Serrano C. (2019) Bluetooth Spy. [Trabajo Fin de Grado] Universidad de Jaén. https://crea.ujaen.es/bitstream/10953.1/11906/1/Memoria_TFM_Espia_Bluetooth.pdf
- Silva, Neif, & Espina, Jane (2006). Computer Ethics in the Information Society. Revista Venezolana de Gerencia, 11(36), 559-580. Retrieved December 21, 2023, from http://ve.scielo.org/scielo.php?script=sci_arttext&pid=S1315-99842006000400004&lng=es&tlng=es.
- Solórzano, E. & Bohórquez, J (2016). Prototype of a parental control for the internet at home, operated from an android device [Trabajo Fin de Grado].
- Tigo Panamá (n.d.). Retrieved from [https://www.tigo.com.pa/empresas/blog/ciberseguridad-en-panama-sepractica]
- ITU. (2020). Global increase in e-waste: more than 21 percent in 2020.
5 years. https://www.itu.int/es/mediacentre/Pages/pr10-2020-global-ewastemonitor.aspx
- Urcuqui L. C. C. García P. M. & Osorio Q. J. L. (2018). Cybersecurity: um enfoque desde la ciencia de datos: (ed.). Editorial Universidad Icesi. https://elibro.net/es/lc/upanama/titulos/120435

- Viñals Blanco, A. (2016). The Connected, mobile, transmedia and multi-support Leisure of young people in the Digital Age. Fonseca, Journal of Communication, 13(13), 99-113. https://doi.org/10.14201/fjc20161399113
- 5th Iberoamerican Conference on Systems, Cybernetics and Informatics.
- National Information Technology Center.
- Latin America and the Caribbean.
- Organization of American States. Meeting June 05 2006.

Printed by Books on Demand GmbH, Norderstedt / Germany